MICHAEL B. JORDAN

ACTOR AND PRODUCER

by Rachel Rose

Minneapolis, Minnesota

Credits
Cover and title page, © Andrea Raffin/Shutterstock; 5, © Joe Seer/Shutterstock; 6, © Variety/Getty Images; 7, © Jamie McCarthy/Getty Images; 9, © Stephen Lovekin/Getty Images; 10, © Cinematic/Alamy Stock Photo; 11, © Album/Alamy Stock Photo; 12, © Kevin Mazur/Getty Images; 13, © Entertainment Pictures/Alamy Stock Photo; 15, © AFF/Alamy Stock Photo; 16, © Album/Alamy Stock Photo; 17, © Willy Sanjuan/ASSOCIATED PRESS; 18, © George Pimentel/Getty Images; 19, © Joe Scarnici/Getty Images; 21, © Karwai Tang/Getty Images; 22T, © Stephen Lovekin/Getty Images; 22M, © Album/Alamy Stock Photo; 22B, © Entertainment Pictures/Alamy Stock Photo.

Bearport Publishing Company Product Development Team
Publisher: Jen Jenson; Director of Product Development: Spencer Brinker; Editorial Director: Allison Juda; Editor: Cole Nelson; Editor: Tiana Tran; Production Editor: Naomi Reich; Art Director: Kim Jones; Designer: Kayla Eggert; Designer: Steve Scheluchin; Production Specialist: Owen Hamlin

Statement on Usage of Generative Artificial Intelligence
Bearport Publishing remains committed to publishing high-quality nonfiction books. Therefore, we restrict the use of generative AI to ensure accuracy of all text and visual components pertaining to a book's subject. See BearportPublishing.com for details.

Library of Congress Cataloging-in-Publication Data

Names: Rose, Rachel, 1968– author.
Title: Michael B. Jordan : actor and producer / Rachel Rose.
Description: Minneapolis, MN : Bearport Publishing Company, 2025. | Series: Bearport biographies | Includes bibliographical references and index.
Identifiers: LCCN 2025001530 (print) | LCCN 2025001531 (ebook) | ISBN 9798895770399 (library binding) | ISBN 9798895774656 (paperback) | ISBN 9798895771563 (ebook)
Subjects: LCSH: Jordan, Michael B. (Michael Bakari), 1987—-Juvenile literature. | African American actors—United States—Biography—Juvenile literature.
Classification: LCC PN2287.J68 R67 2025 (print) | LCC PN2287.J68 (ebook) | DDC 791.4302/8 [B]—dc23/eng/20250117
LC record available at https://lccn.loc.gov/2025001530
LC ebook record available at https://lccn.loc.gov/2025001531

Copyright © 2026 Bearport Publishing Company. All rights reserved. No part of this publication may be reproduced in whole or in part, stored in any retrieval system, or transmitted in any form or by any means, electronic, mechanical, photocopying, recording, or otherwise, without written permission from the publisher. Bearport Publishing is a division of FlutterBee Education Group.

For more information, write to Bearport Publishing, 3500 American Blvd W, Suite 150, Bloomington, MN 55431.

Contents

On the Red Carpet 4

An Early Start 6

Big Breaks 10

Many Roles 14

Way to Wellness 18

More to Come 20

Timeline 22

Glossary 23

Index 24

Read More 24

Learn More Online 24

About the Author 24

On the Red Carpet

Cameras clicked and flashed as Michael B. Jordan walked the carpet at the world **premiere** of his movie *Creed III*. Not only was Michael the star, but he was also the film's **director**. It was his first time taking on this new role. He said it was one of the hardest and the most **rewarding** things he's ever done!

Creed III made more than $275 million in theaters—earning more than both of the Creed movies that came before it.

Michael B. poses like a boxer at the premiere.

An Early Start

Michael Bakari Jordan was born on February 9, 1987, in Santa Ana, California, but his family moved to Newark, New Jersey, when he was very young. Michael's parents wanted to help him succeed in everything he did. When he was 10 years old, his mother **encouraged** him to become a child model. This started his **career** in the spotlight.

Michael B. with his older sister Jamila (left) and younger brother Khalid (right)

Michael's middle name, Bakari, means hopeful in Swahili.

Michael B. with his mother and father.

It wasn't long before modeling led to acting. By age 12, Michael B. had some small roles in popular TV shows, including *Cosby* and *The Sopranos*. Within a few years, he began getting bigger parts. He spent three years playing the character Reggie on the daytime TV drama *All My Children*.

In addition to juggling school and acting, Michael played on his school's basketball team.

Michael B. was invited to **award** shows for his part in *All My Children*.

Big Breaks

In 2013, Michael B. landed his first leading film role in the movie *Fruitvale Station*. He won several awards for his work. Soon after, he got an even bigger break starring in the hit movie *Creed*. Michael spent almost a year training to get in shape to play the part of boxer Adonis Creed.

Fruitvale Station is based on a true story.

Creed tells the story of troubled youth Adonis Creed, who became a famous boxer.

Then, Michael B. was cast as the **villain** Erik Killmonger in the superhero movie *Black Panther*. He wanted the character on the screen to seem real. So, Michael worked hard to show the reasons behind Killmonger's actions. His performance made many fans care about the villain, which was different from most other superhero films.

While filming, Michael B. formed a close friendship with his co-star Chadwick Boseman *(right)*.

Michael B. as Killmonger

Set in a fictional African country and with a mostly Black cast, *Black Panther* celebrated African culture.

Many Roles

As his career grew, Michael B. wanted to help bring more **diversity** to Hollywood. In 2016, he started his own **production company**, Outlier Society. Through this business, Michael has been able to make many films about social issues in the United States. A lot of these movies feature stories that are often overlooked.

Outlier Society makes it a priority to hire a diverse cast and crew for all its projects.

Soon, Michael decided to take on a new challenge—this time behind the camera. In addition to acting and producing, he was ready to try his hand at directing. His first project was a big one. Through Outlier Society, Michael directed the 2023 film *Creed III*. Having starred in the first two movies of the series, he felt prepared to take charge of the story.

Michael B. spoke with other actor-directors for advice on how to balance the two demanding jobs.

Michael B. got a star on the Hollywood Walk of Fame in March 2023.

Way to Wellness

Making movies isn't the only work Michael B. cares about. He often speaks out about mental health issues, especially among Black men. The superstar also works with different **organizations** to promote fitness as a tool for both physical and mental well-being. For Michael, taking care of the mind and body go hand in hand.

Michael B.'s production company runs **mentorship** programs to help guide young people.

Michael B. was in a commercial for a fitness drink. The ad aimed to get people active.

More to Come

Michael B. started his career at a young age. With talent and hard work, he has become a movie star, a producer, and a director. Along the way, he has strived to help others and create more diversity in Hollywood. Still, Michael B. has more he wants to do—and he will work hard to get it done!

After his success with *Creed III*, Michael B. plans to continue directing.

Timeline

Here are some key dates in Michael B.'s life.

1987 — Born on February 9

1997 — Becomes a child model

1999 — Gets first acting job

2013 — Lands lead role in *Fruitvale Station*

2015 — Stars as Adonis Creed in *Creed*

2016 — Starts production company, Outlier Society

2018 — Plays villain in *Black Panther*

2023 — Directs, produces, and stars in *Creed III*

Glossary

award a prize for being the best at something

career the job a person has for a long period of time

director a person who tells actors what to do

diversity the presence of many different kinds of people

encouraged gave support or help to someone

mentorship guidance given from people who have more experience

organizations groups of people with common interests or goals

premiere the first public showing of a movie or show

production company a business that makes movies, video games, or TV shows

rewarding giving a good feeling or a sense of satisfaction

villain an evil or bad person

Index

actor 16
All My Children 8-9
Black Panther 12-13, 22
Boseman, Chadwick 12
Cosby 8
Creed 4, 10-11, 16, 20, 22
director 4, 16, 20, 22
Fruitvale Station 10, 22
Killmonger, Erik 12-13
mental health 18
model 6, 8, 22
Outlier Society 14, 22
producer 16, 18, 20, 22
villain 12, 22

Read More

Abdo, Kenny. *The Making of Black Panther (Blockbusters)*. Minneapolis: Abdo Zoom, 2024.

Sipperley, Keli. *Michael B. Jordan (Celebrity Bios)*. Mankato, MN: Apex Editions, 2025.

Learn More Online

1. Go to **FactSurfer.com** or scan the QR code below.
2. Enter "**Michael B. Jordan**" into the search box.
3. Click on the cover of this book to see a list of websites.

About the Author

Rachel Rose is a writer and coach who lives in San Francisco. Her favorite books to write are about people who lead inspiring lives.